Advance Praise for After Words

Shirley Brewer's *After Words* is a testament to the spirit of compassionate community that embodies the best of Baltimore and all of us. In the face of tragedy, she reaches out as a loving neighbor to address the inexplicable: the senseless murder of Stephen Pitcairn, a researcher whose dream of becoming a doctor and alleviating others' pain is abruptly cut short one night in Charles Village. In sharing her work with members of the Pitcairn family, the author gives voice to the lost and offers solace to the bereaved. *After Words* is proof of the power of words—to express outrage, to comfort and to heal.

> —Ned Balbo, author of *The Trials of Edgar Poe and Other Poems* (Story Line Press, 2010), awarded the 2010 Donald Justice Prize and the 2012 Poets' Prize. He teaches at Loyola University, Baltimore, MD.

Shirley Brewer and I constantly walk the walk Stephen Pitcairn was taking when he met his murderers; it's where we live. Brewer walks the walk in a second way—via her powerful, gut-wrenching, brave words. Brewer's wise, beautifully crafted book, with its moving foreword by the victim's mother, images the unimaginable in a way that teaches me how to think about the unthinkable and, as Brewer says in the opening poem, to *give thanks for the days/you walked among us*.

Readers familiar with Shirley Brewer's wry, witty, often slightly amused poetic voice will not hear it here. Instead they will hear the voices of Pitcairn, his mother, Reggie Higgins and, yes, even the knife.

> —Poet Clarinda Harriss is Professor Emerita of Towson University and Director of Brick House Books, Inc., Baltimore, MD.

Shirley Brewer's stunning poems give voice to an urban Baltimore community struck by crime, to the young victim following his death, to his grieving mother, and to the neighbor - Reggie Higgins - who held and comforted Stephen in his last minutes of life. They reflect, in beautifully crafted lines, the horror of violence, the depth and duration of grieving, the incredible kindness of a stranger and, most of all, the tenderness, anger, love and wit of the young victim in messages sent after his death. Brewer brings us to the edge of an abyss and holds our collective hand.

> —Margaret S. Mullins divides her time between rural Maryland and downtown Baltimore. She is the author of the chapbook *Family Constellation* (Finishing Line Press, 2012) and the editor of *Manorborn: The Water Issue* (Abecedarian Press, 2009).

In *After Words*, Shirley Brewer has written with great empathy a gorgeous elegy to Stephen Pitcairn, his family and to the citizens of Baltimore. The collection of poems in many voices, most written in compressed couplets, documents Pitcairn's murder with a lyric intensity that only poetry can achieve. Brewer is working here in the company of other poetic witnesses: Muriel Rukeyser's *Book of the Dead,* Carolyn Forché's poems on El Salvador, C.D. Wright's recent *One With Others*. And, yes, there are other voices as there are other atrocities. And we, *In quiet, simple moments,* encounter Brewer's large-hearted offering, which enables us to participate with our own *small gesture* of healing.

> —Jennifer Wallace teaches at the Maryland Institute College of Art in Baltimore, MD. She is a poetry editor at *The Cortland Review*, and a founding editor of Toadlily Press. Her new book, *It Can Be Solved By Walking*, was published in 2012 by CityLit Press.

AFTER WORDS

Shirley J. Brewer

Apprentice House
Loyola University Maryland
Baltimore, Maryland

First Edition
Printed in the United States of America
ISBN: 978-1-934074-82-4

Cover design by: Alexa Lombardi
Cover photo by: Bonnie Schupp

Published by Apprentice House

Apprentice House
Loyola University Maryland
4501 N. Charles Street
Baltimore, MD 21210
410.617.5265 · 410.617.2198 (fax)
www.ApprenticeHouse.com
info@ApprenticeHouse.com

Beautiful, beautiful, beautiful
Beautiful boy
Beautiful, beautiful, beautiful
Beautiful boy
   —*John Lennon*

Acknowledgements

I want to thank these special people who read all or parts of *After Words*, and offered their insights and feedback: Margaret S. Mullins, Dean Bartoli Smith, Jim Taylor, Ned Balbo, Jennifer Wallace, Clarinda Harriss, Barbara Morrison, Laura Shovan, Kathleen Hellen, David Ettlin and Bonnie Schupp.

Words alone cannot express my gratitude to Gwen Pitcairn, who gave her full support to this project, and shared with me many memories of her remarkable son. Thank you, Gwen, from my heart to yours.

Contents

Preface

Stephen Bradley Pitcairn, a native of Tequesta, Florida, and a Johns Hopkins researcher, looked forward to attending medical school and becoming a doctor. He loved his work, and the many friends he'd made during his year in Baltimore.

Stephen's life ended when he was stabbed in the heart during a robbery on St. Paul Street on Sunday night, July 25, 2010.

I did not know Stephen Pitcairn when he was alive. When I saw his picture in the news, his open joyful face touched me to the core. His murder took place only one block from my home. In the middle of that week, I attended a memorial service for Stephen at the site of his murder. I met Reggie Higgins, who held and comforted Stephen during his final moments. One of my neighbors suggested I write a poem to Stephen's family.

A few days later, I wrote "Offering" and sent it to the Pitcairn family. Shortly after, I received a lovely note of thanks from Stephen's mother, Gwen Pitcairn. I was deeply touched that this woman who had just lost her only son would take time to write me. We began a correspondence. I continued to follow the story of Stephen's murder and its aftermath. In late August of 2010, much to my surprise, I wrote another poem, this one in Stephen's voice. It seemed to me that he had more to say, and I was just listening and writing down his words. More poems followed—in Stephen's voice, in Reggie's voice, in Gwen's voice.

I felt Stephen's beauty in every poem I wrote. May *After Words* soothe and heal, and help keep Stephen's memory alive.

Gwen Pitcairn had lost three babies to miscarriages before Stephen was born. He was her miracle child, a gift. She has written, for *After Words*, a moving dedication to her son. I would like to add my own dedication – to Gwen Pitcairn and the Pitcairn family for their unimaginable loss, to Reggie Higgins for his immense and loving heart, and to every parent who has suffered the loss of a child.

Shirley J. Brewer
July, 2012

Stephen in Japan, a country he loved.

Dedicated to Stephen Bradley Pitcairn
July 27, 1986 – July 25, 2010

My son and friend
who was and continues to be
a never-ending source of inspiration

Words seem inadequate when I try to describe Stephen and explain the depths of how much he means to me, his family, friends and acquaintances. Stephen was always striving to obtain as much knowledge as he possibly could, with the goal of living his life to the absolute fullest. His presence always left one aware of his warmth, kindness, compassion and sincerity of spirit. Stephen touched lives wherever he went and affected people in such a positive way. His energy for life and enthusiasm to share was powerful and far-reaching. From his hometown of Tequesta, Florida to Kalamazoo, to Tokyo and lastly to Baltimore, his life made a difference to others and he will never be forgotten. I found a Skype conversation that we had while he studied abroad in Japan during his junior year of college. His words now seem so profound:

Mom, you know I believe that I have been given a lot in life
And I want to give a lot
And at the end to have left some small mark that people will remember
To me that will be a life well-lived

Oh Stephen, you left a small mark and so much more! May this collection of poems leave an even bigger mark because of your absence.

The world lost a beautiful soul on July 25th 2010, and heaven gained another shining star. I love you forever and always.

—*Your loving Madre, Okassan, Mom. xo*

Thank you, Shirley, for sharing your gift of poetry in honor of Stephen's memory, and thanks to everyone who made this publication a reality.

—*Gwen E. Pitcairn, August, 2012*

Offering

Poem for Stephen Pitcairn
from the residents of Charles Village
July 31, 2010

We felt the knife too, an awful
stab in our collective heart,

a pain so deep we have spent
sleepless hours thinking of you.

We want to bring you back—
our neighbor—your handsome face

once more animated, curious, kind.
We want to present you,

whole and vibrant, to your mother,
so connected to you

she listened to your birth cries
twenty-four years ago,

then heard over the phone
the unimaginable agony of your death.

A full moon blessed Baltimore that night
you stepped off the bus at Penn Station,

inhaled the balmy air,
your legs stiff from a long ride.

Always a walker, you made the choice
to travel by foot the last mile home.

A call to your mom wrapped your journey
in family and warmth.

Perhaps you spoke about your weekend
visit with your sisters in New York,

your plans to celebrate
your upcoming birthday with friends.

Evil appeared on St. Paul Street,
penetrated the neighborhood we love.

You pleaded for humanity.
Evil attacked.

In the darkness, a man emerged,
a gentle neighbor who held you,

comforted you. Oh, Stephen, please know
Reggie Higgins was all of us, on our knees in the street.

Stephen Pitcairn—son, brother, researcher, friend—
dedicated, promising, brilliant, fun,

we did not save you.
You died in Charles Village.

We cannot change what happened; even
the moon wept, her face a mother's wound.

Yesterday, your family in Florida buried you.
Did they spit out *Baltimore?*

We who also grieve your loss
wonder, Stephen, what can we offer you:

a world without monsters, without scars,
a village without crime?

We offer you resolve, the will
to make good change.

We offer you a safe haven in our hearts,
a warm place at our dinner tables.

We offer you this poem, a space
in each lovely Charles Village garden.

We offer you a walk on a gorgeous day,
a meal at the Paper Moon.

Most of all, we promise to hold the hand
of everyone who needs us.

Stephen, in your duffel bag
that night you carried your dreams.

If every Charles Village resident
holds on to your life vision,

imagine the powerful impact
on this hazy, damaged world.

We give thanks for the days
you walked among us.

We give thanks to your parents
for sharing you.

In quiet, simple moments,
life moves forward:

small gestures, greetings, the way
we touch the flowers.

Stephen Pitcairn, your light continues,
brighter than a full Charles Village moon.

Slain

—August 25, 2010

I miss small joys: oysters
on the half shell, a good joke.

I want years to explore
all the stops on my personal map.

Give me the chance to celebrate
my twenty-fourth birthday.

Is it too much to ask
for one piece of chocolate cake?

I grieve for my parents, my sisters,
my co-workers, my friends—
the light they lost when I died.

My mother heard my final cries
over the phone—*Mom,*
the last word I spoke.

I need time for embraces, hugs,
a long exuberant farewell.

I forgive the pair who gouged my heart;
make them understand what they did.

Thank you, kind stranger,
who held me in the street.

I did not know your name;
I could barely move my lips.

Blood flowed from my wound,
soaking both of us.

I felt your comfort—your voice
calmed my final breath.

Goodbye, dear ones, I'll be off now,
the youngest doctor in the angel crowd;
they gave me an instant medical degree.

Look for me in the gallant
green-garbed full moon, my grin
an oasis in the night sky.

In tranquil moments, listen to nature:
birds, cicadas, a butterfly wing.
In their music, my heart still beats.

Lifeline

—September 25, 2010, my mom's birthday

Death by knife, unfair
separation from matter,

from all that matters—the safe
cocoon of family, friends.

I long to comfort my mom,
who weeps every night in my room.

If I could look in a mirror
right now, what would I see?

No one says: *Death
becomes you.*

The dead cannot speak—
both lungs and larynx lost.

If another language thrives here,
I have not yet learned it.

My words still shine like candles
tossed into the white cauldron of moon.

I'm restless, feverish—so much
unsaid, undone.

How do I relinquish
the parts of me that will not die?

This lonely country could be illusion,
except I remember my casket

lowered into the ground,
severing me

from my sisters drenched in black.
Let me undie,

ride the Bolt bus back to Baltimore.
I miss my human connections:

a cup of coffee with my buddies, one more
phone call home.

My Mother Speaks

—October 25, 2010

Sun, unbearable star,
illuminates the sky—

another crushing day
without you on this Earth.

Blue mornings blur my vision,
conjure your lost eyes.

The knife severed two
hearts, left mine

a wounded sparrow
shuddering inside me.

When sleep will not come
I call your dead phone,

your voice an absence
my ears grieve;

the silence keeps getting
louder and louder.

My path broken,
your departure so abrupt—

the steps of your journey
alive in my mind:

My beautiful boy,
you leaped into this world,

became a man, your gifts
a salve, a healing force.

That last night, you spoke with passion
about your research, a chance to serve.

When you ran into evil,
it could not stand your bliss.

Stephen, send me a light,
a portion of moon,

something I can embrace,
a way to touch you, Son.

Each time I breathe, my chest
feels the blade.

O Sewa Ni Narimashita

—Thanksgiving Day, 2010

In a realm too new
to feel like home,

I give thanks for 8,758
days spent on Earth,

where I walked with purpose
into the promising wind.

Life is a garment
worn for a short time;

mine came apart in the sudden
slash of a knife

on moon-drenched St. Paul Street
in the heart of Baltimore.

I've savored a good meal,
cooking with my mom,

recipes, dinners, dessert.
When my family gathers today,

I want to hold hands
with each of them—I miss their touch.

Hug me with words, I call
from this faraway space. You

who survive me, talk to me;
keep me in a living place.

Replay my memories,
my year in Japan—

the incredible sky, sunsets,
layers of blood orange.

Oyasumi nasai,
Good night.

O sewa ni narimashita,
Thanks for everything.

Reggie Higgins Speaks

—Christmas Day, 2010

In the heart of winter,
people swarm to the malls,

search for presents, while I
relive the night my life changed:

an ordinary Sunday in July, the moon
a brilliant pearl in the Baltimore sky.

I heard a loud cry, an anguished scream—
sounds so raw they resonate in my sleep.

I ran outside, the street lamp dark.
A young man lay by the curb—a hole

in his chest, a rush of blood I could not stop.
I held him as if he were my own, never mind

the different shades of our skin—
both of us red in the moonlight.

I cradled his head, he called out *Mom*
before dying in my arms.

I did not know Stephen Pitcairn until
his last moments on Earth. If I can believe

my presence soothed him on his journey,
then I received the best gift.

I held him in the summer night;
no one should die alone.

A Message from Stephen

—February 25, 2011

No January poem—like you,
the dead retreat in winter.

I've taken time to reflect
on my murder, the quick

jab of a knife that ended
my journey on Earth.

I miss my life,
when each day unfolded—

a thrilling new project to tackle
even when

the ladder trembles,
and you spill nails

all over the floor. You laugh,
start over, relish a fresh chance.

From this height, I can see
chaos in your cluttered world,

the culture drowning you
in noise. Don't listen.

Go your sweet way, follow
the thread of your passion.

How do you know
when you must let go? You don't.

I did not anticipate
violence that summer night.

After the attack, I looked up
at the full moon. Her sweet face

witnessed blood leaving my body,
a wound I could not wish away.

Before I closed my eyes
for the last time, I heard

the gentle voice of a man
who offered me comfort.

Hear me, dear ones, honor
your gifts, the magic. Live well.

A smile is a permanent fire
you light from within.

To My Killers

—April 3, 2011

Did you feel anything
when you took my life?

Your blade broke through
skin and muscle, tore my young heart.

Marked with my blood, you ran
like rabid dogs into the moon-carved night.

You carried away my wallet, my phone—
possessions I had already offered.

I imagine your hearts
black canyons unable to bear

the lightness you heard in my voice
as I talked to my mom.

The rage of all you never knew
exploded in your brains.

Your knife spoke, its upward thrust
a curse—your lives a bad list:

misdeeds, the tumbling fall
into the cesspool of the world.

Do you wake up with remorse? What if
you could start over,

return to your infant blankets,
gaze into the faces of mothers who loved you?

What might have changed
the paths you followed?

Your awful choices
severed my journey.

One year ago today, I saw my mom
for the last time. I want to go back,

comfort her. When you kill a son,
you kill his mother too.

One Year After My Murder

—July 25, 2011

Mom, if only you knew how many ways
I've tried to reach you.

I've sent you signals
from every star,

made a pact with the moon
to glow more luminous in your sky,

bartered with the sun
for extra light on your path.

I regret you had to hear
my death over the phone—

our last conversation cut short
by a swift and ugly knife.

My plans and hopes
drowned in my blood on St. Paul Street.

An unnecessary end.
When I reflect in this quiet,

a galaxy of glorious memories
appears, and Mom, you're always there:

all the talks and walks we shared.
Even after I left home—

Michigan, Japan, Baltimore—
we kept our close connection.

You made my heart beat;
I listen to your heart.

Did they think a knife
was enough to part us?

I accomplished much
on Earth—I see that now.

On this first anniversary of my murder,
I give thanks to you, Mom,

for the gift of my life.
I believe I lived it well.

Invisible, my hand rests
steady on your shoulder.

After Words

—*October 25, 2011*

Cold autumn rain
blurs the landscape.

The trial over,
a sentence handed down—

my mom returns home,
her suitcase the lightest burden

she bears. Murder
leaves a heavy space,

the full moon
a circular loss in the sky.

Now, I appear only in photographs
I hope won't wrinkle or fade.

My family and friends
will always weep.

I want to comfort them,
be my own ghost this Halloween—

show up at their doors,
make them smile again.

Death can't take everything;
I know I mattered.

After words, my heat
still warms the earth.

Moon, Tree, Knife

I
Moon

> I was full that night,
> my favorite phase.
>
> Stephen looked up at me,
> a beacon to guide him home,
>
> my gold surface a blessing.
> What I offered was not enough.
>
> When he fell,
> my light revealed his blood.
>
> Stephen gazed skyward,
> struggled for breath,
>
> saw my perfect face.
> I hope I gave him
> one last burst of joy.

II
Tree

> In summer, my foliage
> provides a respite from heat,
>
> the sun's fervor. I am
> a sanctuary of nature in the city.
>
> That night, my roots trembled
> when two people killed a boy,

my shadows hiding
their brutal attack.

He died beneath my branches.
I could do nothing.

I wanted to embrace Stephen
and the neighbor who held him,
wrap them both in my healing green.

III
Knife

My blade ended Stephen's life.
It was not my choice.

Men created me
for good deeds:

slicing apples, whittling
an animal from a piece of wood.

At the trial, lawyers held me aloft;
I felt the loathing in everyone's eyes.

The killers who used me that night
expressed no remorse.

Dear family, whose lives
I slashed, forgive me
for the loss of your beautiful boy.

Two Years After My Murder

—July 25, 2012

When death is fresh,
everyone pays attention.

A face in the news,
flowers at the murder site—

grief a sound
that blocks out the sun.

Months pass; the moon
returns to fullness.

The faucet of sorrow—
once a force—slows.

Family and friends
camouflage their pain,

suffer in the dark
silence of memories.

A knife stopped my heart
on a summer night.

I can't forget that knife;
a weapon trumps a dream.

Who will trust
the voices of the dead?

This strange language
may not be heard,

my journey from *I am*
to *I was*—too abrupt,

my blood mixing
with the litter of the street.

I felt the knife go in.
I was scared.

The energy of last moments
is a story unwritten.

Time is fleeting;
color lasts forever.

I live on in blue,
a doctor of sky.

Offering: A Refrain

In quiet, simple moments,
life moves forward:

small gestures, greetings, the way
we touch the flowers.

Stephen Pitcairn, your light continues,
brighter than a full Charles Village moon.

Remember me, speak my name.
When the moon tugs at my sleeve,
When the body of water is raised and
becomes the body of light,
Remember me, speak my name.
  —*Charles Wright, "Homage to Paul Cézanne"*

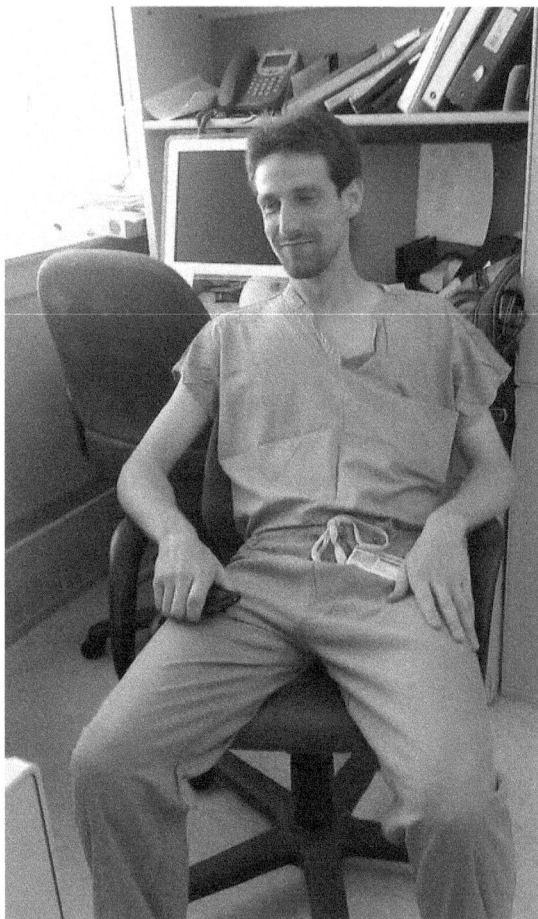

A few weeks before Stephen's murder, at a time when he was shadowing a surgeon.

Stephen's Personal Statement

This *Personal Statement* is an essay Stephen wrote as part of his application to medical school. His dream was to be accepted into Johns Hopkins (his first choice) as a medical student and to become a physician.

—Shirley J. Brewer

———————

Please look on me favorably, I said, bowing deeply as I concluded my first self-introduction to the Orthopedics faculty at Nihon University in Tokyo, Japan. This greeting marked the beginning of a yearlong clinical and research internship with the university hospital, one of the most rewarding and challenging experiences of my life. The following story has been instrumental in my decision to become a doctor.

The notion to pursue a career in medicine came during the summer between my first and second year of college. I struggled through my freshman year but garnered an internship at a joint replacement research lab in West Palm Beach, Florida. It was my first real exposure to the medical field. I was instantly fascinated. Performing basic x-ray analyses and implant retrieval gave me my first insight into evidence-based medicine. I was beginning to see how a doctor could use patients' histories to develop new procedures and devices. In my dissections of cadavers I became intrigued with the intricate, if sometimes grotesque, anatomy of the human body. I was struck by how the science I had studied in school became increasingly relevant. But it was more than just the research that drew me; it was the diversity of disciplines the field offered, as well as the tangible goal of improving the quality of a person's life, in which I found a calling.

This was also when I started learning Japanese. I became enthralled with the language and the intellectual challenge it presented. With a borrowed textbook and the aid of several

Japanese research fellows, I made rapid progress. I found a renewed discipline and focus for my studies. That summer culminated in a three-week sojourn through Japan. By the time second year classes rolled around, I knew what I wanted. Without reconciling one for the other, I was determined to pursue both Japanese and medicine.

My second year flew by as I finished my premedical coursework. Passing a language exam qualified me for a yearlong study-abroad program in Tokyo. The summer before leaving for Japan, I was privileged to intern with an orthopedics lab at Massachusetts General Hospital in Boston. In addition to my classes at Waseda University, I secured an internship with the Department of Orthopedics at Nihon University. I was living my dream and combining my two passions: experiencing medicine and experiencing medicine in Japan. Interacting with doctors, communicating with patients—all while navigating the subtleties of a Japanese hospital—provided daily stimulation and led to a deeper cultural and medical understanding.

My experience at Nihon University was typified by my relationship with a young osteosarcoma patient named Akiko. She initially presented with a Stage II, rapidly metastasizing, tumor in her tibia. I was privy to her consultation, witnessed her chemotherapy, observed the removal of her tumor, and the insertion of a total knee arthroplasty. I closely followed her recovery, all the while being humbled by the opportunity to understand this life-altering experience through the eyes of a 13-year-old schoolgirl.

The essence of our relationship was evident one evening during a few free minutes after rounds in the pediatric ward. I saw her folding paper cranes at her bed and asked if she could teach me how. We chatted about boys and what she wanted to be when she grew up. She said the chemotherapy hurt and that she sometimes felt lonely at night in the hospital. She didn't mind having a smooth, bald head and was delighted I could come see her. I felt truly privileged to have been able to bring her a few moments of happiness. I learned much more than how to fold paper cranes.

In many ways I view my relationship with Akiko as a personification of my fascination with Japan. Connecting with her was an opportunity to reach out, through the nuances of a distinctive language and culture, to find something precious in someone that would have otherwise been unreachable. The gravity of her medical situation brought home the uniqueness of getting to know her. It confirmed my drive to become a physician.

Nihon University also gave me the opportunity to examine the underlying biology of tissue regeneration and the great potential of stem cell therapy. In the project that became my senior thesis, I performed surgery on rats and completed detailed microbiological analyses of the mechanisms of angiogenesis. Following this inspiration, I decided to deepen my knowledge of medical biology and sharpen my laboratory techniques in my post-baccalaureate years. I am currently working at The Johns Hopkins University School of Medicine studying the physical and biological effects of hypoxic microenvironments in breast cancer tumors and how this relates to cancer metastasis. Contributing to the science behind medical progress gives me a tremendous feeling of accomplishment and purpose.

My commitment to both medicine and the Japanese language has enriched my ways of thinking and given me a vehicle for communication. I long for a career that allows me to explore my intellectual curiosities while at the same time interacting with and aiding others. I find a life devoted to medicine to be formidable, but ultimately fulfilling. Thus, it is with great conviction that I seek to acquire a medical education.

—*Stephen B. Pitcairn*

Stephen Pitcairn
Scholarship Fund

Johns Hopkins Medical School is committed to making sure Stephen's work lives on. They have established the Stephen B. Pitcairn Scholarship Fund, and invite your support. All contributions are welcome. No amount is too small. This fund will help pay tuition for young men and women who—like Stephen— aspire to become doctors. Donations can be mailed to:

Stephen B. Pitcairn Scholarship Fund
Johns Hopkins School of Medicine
100 N. Charles Street   Suite 200
Baltimore, MD 21201-3805

You may also donate online:
http://www.hopkinsmedicine.org/som/alumni/support/
stephen_pitcairn_memorial_scholarship_fund.html

Be sure to designate the gift for the Stephen Pitcairn Scholarship in the "Other" section. Thank you for your support in Stephen's memory.

About Shirley Brewer

Shirley J. Brewer is an educator and workshop facilitator. Her poetry has appeared in *The Cortland Review, Comstock Review, Passager, Free Lunch, Innisfree Poetry Journal, Pearl, Evening Street Review,* and other publications. Her poetry chapbook, *A Little Breast Music*, was published in 2008 by Passager Books (Baltimore). Shirley lives in the Baltimore community of Charles Village.

Talented writers, innovative students, fresh minds at work.

Apprentice House is the country's only campus-based, student-staffed book publishing company. Directed by professors and industry professionals, it is a nonprofit activity of the Communication Department at Loyola University Maryland.

Using state-of-the-art technology and an experiential learning model of education, Apprentice House publishes books in untraditional ways. This dual responsibility as publishers and educators creates an unprecedented collaborative environment among faculty and students, while teaching tomorrow's editors, designers, and marketers.

Outside of class, progress on book projects is carried forth by the AH Book Publishing Club, a co-curricular campus organization supported by Loyola University Maryland's Office of Student Activities.

Eclectic and provocative, Apprentice House titles intend to entertain as well as spark dialogue on a variety of topics. Financial contributions to sustain the press's work are welcomed. Contributions are tax deductible to the fullest extent allowed by the IRS.

To learn more about Apprentice House books or to obtain submission guidelines, please visit www.ApprenticeHouse.com.

Apprentice House
Communication Department
Loyola University Maryland
4501 N. Charles Street
Baltimore, MD 21210
Ph: 410-617-5265 • Fax: 410-617-2198
info@apprenticehouse.com • www.apprenticehouse.com

www.ingramcontent.com/pod-product-compliance
Lightning Source LLC
Chambersburg PA
CBHW071438040426
42445CB00012BA/1392